De l'obscurité à la lumière

story:

Jennifer Degenhardt

illustrator:

Juliette Chattaway

translator:

Theresa Marrama

editors:

Françoise Piron & Nicole Piron

Copyright © 2023 Jennifer Degenhardt (Puentes)
All rights reserved.
ISBN: 978-1-956594-43-0

This story is for all who experience challenges with their mental health.
May you find your ray of sunshine.

AUTHOR'S NOTE

Hello!

Thank you for taking the time to read this message before you start reading. It's important that you know what you might find in the pages so you can make a reasonable choice whether or not to dive in.

This story deals with inner turmoil and associated dark thoughts, up to and including those of self-harm. I did not write this story to be triggering to anyone, but rather - as always - to provide an opportunity for discussion. It is my hope that by sharing a story that is based on feelings that I have had personally, that I can help with the discussion about self-harm, suicidal thoughts and the spiral that the human mind can get itself into. Yes, you read that right: I have struggled with depression and delicate mental health for many years, which ultimately led to some really negative thinking. While it is not a time in my life that I wish to revisit, I am grateful for the experience, as it has changed the way I view everything in life.

The first and best thing I did was to ask for help. And I didn't just ask one person, I asked many. Family and friends were there for me, as I know that family and friends would be for anyone, if the person in need simply asks for help.

This story is meant to serve as a jumping-off point to talk about mental health and to provide one look into the anxiety that some experience. Furthermore, since each person's journey is different, the novel ends with possibility. In no way does the ending mean to suggest that struggles such as these can be easily taken care of with an ice cream, a flower or even a puppy. Still, I wanted to end with some hope for better days - like the ones I am so fortunate enough to experience now.

The subject matter is difficult. Please read with care.

-Jen Degenhardt
September 2023

You aren't going to feel this way forever, you know.

The mind has thoughts, and those thoughts control your feelings.

It will all be okay in the end. If it's not okay, it's not the end.

Try to think positively. Everything in life – including the bad – is temporary.

I imagine that your path in life will be a little difficult for a while, but it won't be forever. Everything will get better.

Remember: your thoughts control your feelings. And you can change your thoughts.

REMERCIEMENTS

Having had this story in mind for a while, I started it on the plane on a return flight from California, I think it was. I had done the preparation, taken the notes and had begun writing furiously. And then somehow, I deleted the file. Like, really deleted it, not just in file purgatory. Ugh.

But I had already hired the artist. Juliet Chattaway was still in elementary school when I asked her to draw a teenager in a hoodie, in a bedroom with one window. I then asked her to alter the drawings a bit at a time (I don't want to give it away!), so they too, could be part of the story. Juliet understood my vision exactly, even when I might not always have been so clear. It is a pleasure and an honor to work with student artists like Juliet. They are offered a unique opportunity, and I get to help them realize that "business" doesn't have to be scary. It's a win-win. Many, many thanks to Juliet for her awesome artwork, but also for her patience. Due to - well, life - this novel took longer than I anticipated to get published. Thank you, Juliet!

You are reading this version in French thanks to Theresa Marrama, my business partner and French teacher, who was responsible for the translation; and Françoise Piron and her mother, Nicole Piron who tackled the copyediting and making the language as fluid and comprehensible as possible. Thank you all, for helping this message get to even more readers.

I owe the following people a huge debt of gratitude (and if you're reading this, or any of my books, so do you. 😉) If not for these people to whom I reached out for help those few years ago, I may not have had the opportunity to write this story - or any others for that matter. I am grateful to each of you. Thank you.

Sarah Jessup & Robert Allen
Celia Bartholomew & John Bartholomew
Angela Degenhardt
Claire Degrigrio
Tara Allen & José Salazar
Amy Salvin Collins
Wendy Perrotti
Patti Nietsch

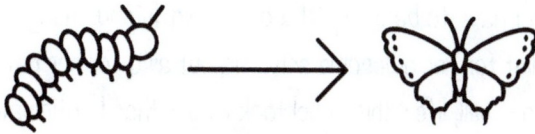

Just when the caterpillar thought the world was over, it became a butterfly...

-proverb

Dans une maison...

ou un appartement...

ou un condo...

La tante frappe à la porte.

La tante entrouvre la porte. Ari est par terre dans une chambre sombre, près du lit.

La tante ouvre la porte un peu plus.

Oui, tatie. Ça va bien.
Enfin, plus ou moins bien.

Laisse-moi ouvrir le store pour que le soleil entre.

OK, Ari. Je dois sortir pendant une heure. Tu veux venir avec moi ? On peut acheter tes bonbons favoris comme d'habitude...

OK. Tu veux vraiment pas venir avec moi ? Je veux pas te laisser.

Ça va. T'inquiète pas. Il va rien se passer pendant une heure.

Non. J'ai besoin de rien.

Ari, tu vas pas toujours te sentir comme ça, tu sais.

Ça va passer Tu verras. À toute à l'heure. Repose-toi.

OK. C'est seulement une heure. Ma tante a confiance en moi. Elle me dit que tout va bien se passer, que je vais pas me sentir toujours comme ça. Mais je sais pas...

23

Bien sûr que tu sais pas. Tu sais rien. Et tu sais rien de l'avenir. C'est moi qui en sais plus que toi.

Non. C'était pas de ma faute. J'ai rien fait de mal.

Mais j'ai pas demandé de payer pour un entraînement si cher. J'aurais préféré m'entraîner à un niveau inférieur.

Non ! C'est pas de ma faute. Mais oui, je veux continuer mon sport. J'ai adoré gagner. Et je gagnais. J'aimais quand tout le monde me regardait gagner.

Tu étais un exemple de perfection chaque fois que tu participais, c'est vrai. Tu voulais cette perfection, et ta famille aussi, n'est-ce pas ? Ta famille était parfaite jusqu'à...

Oui. Je voulais continuer. Je voulais m'améliorer. Je voulais participer au niveau suivant. Mais je connaissais pas le coût... et le coût final...

Oui, JE SAIS. JE SAIS ! C'EST VRAI que je savais. Et oui, je voulais continuer. Je voulais tout.

Et ton père le voulait aussi pour toi. Il voulait un meilleur avenir pour toi. Mais il pouvait pas payer, et il voulait que tu sois une personne heureuse.... Pour cette raison, c'est ta faute.

39

Mais avant qu'il puisse le faire, le client a parlé à la police. Et puis il y a eu l'arrestation... Parce que ton père était alors un criminel.

42

43

45

47

Ari se met à pleurer.

49

Ma famille ! Je veux être avec ma famille !

Je veux que ma vie soit comme avant. Je veux mes parents avec moi et je veux que le seul problème soit un examen en sciences ou la prochaine compétition.

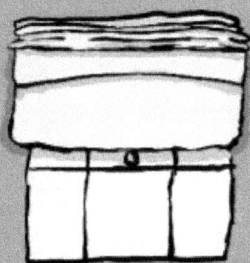

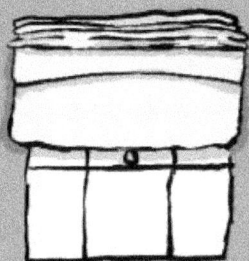

Tu as travaillé si fort que tu t'es blessé. Ensuite, tes parents ont dû payer encore plus d'argent : au centre d'entraînement et à l'hôpital. L'argent qu'ils avaient pas...

58

Ne me reproche rien. Tu es pas réel. C'est moi qui ai le contrôle...

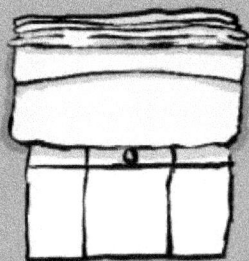

64

65

Je veux pas être un fardeau pour les autres, ni pour mes parents, ni pour ma tante. Je veux m'échapper. Je te demande de m'aider...

67

68

« Je veux ma maman ! »
Qui est-ce que tu appelles ? Ta mère va pas échapper à l'abîme mental où elle se trouve avant que ton père sorte de prison.

Oh! Mon pauvre papa. Il est en prison. Et ma maman...

73

J'ai besoin de prendre mes médicaments quelquefois. Ils m'aident.

79

Tout était de ma faute ! Tout est de ma faute . OUHHHHHH ! J'en peux plus. Je veux me faire du mal pour la dernière fois.

Ari pleure.

Ari prend la boîte de médicaments. On n'entend que des sanglots. Les sanglots d'une personne en détresse. Une personne qui n'a plus de forces...

Ari tient la boîte de médicaments et s'effondre soudain.

Beaucoup de temps s'écoule.

La tante rentre avec un carton dans les mains.

Il n'y a pas de réponse. La seule chose qu'on entend, c'est le bruit que fait le chiot dans le carton.

ouaf, ouaf !

Tais-toi, petit! Tu es une surprise pour Ari...

Il n'y a pas de réponse. La seule chose qu'on entend, c'est le bruit que fait le chiot dans le carton.

La tante pose le carton avec le chiot et court vers Ari.

Les yeux d'Ari s'ouvrent
légèrement.

97

Ari, dis-moi. Est-ce que tu as pris ces médicaments ? Je dois savoir.

Non, tatie. Je les ai pas pris.

101

Ari, tu es responsable de rien. Ces choses arrivent dans la vie. Ton père est un adulte, et il a pris ses propres décisions.

Mais il a volé à ce client pour payer les frais de mon entraînement. Et à cause de ce crime, ma maman a commencé à boire de plus en plus...

Tes parents ont pris leurs décisions. Ce sont des adultes. Tu n'es pas encore adulte.

Espérons qu'ils tiendront compte de ce qui s'est passé et qu'ils seront plus conscients de leurs décisions à l'avenir.

Ari, rappelle-toi que tes pensées contrôlent tes sentiments.

À ce moment-là, le chiot commence à aboyer.

Quand j'étais jeune,
j'avais un chien qui
s'appelait Lumière.

Il m'a beaucoup aidé pendant une période difficile de ma vie. J'ai pensé qu'une amie comme elle pourrait t'être utile.

Oh, tatie !
Laisse-moi le voir !

La tante prend le carton et l'ouvre. Le chiot saute et va directement voir Ari.

Tatie, merci ! Elle est vraiment adorable.

Comment tu vas l'appeler ? Quelque chose qui te rappelle pourquoi c'est ton amie...

Athéna. Je vais l'appeler Athéna. Athéna était la déesse de la sagesse. Le nom va beaucoup m'aider.

Rappelle-toi cette maxime, « Tout est bien qui finit bien. Si ce n'est pas bien, ce n'est pas la fin. »

119

C'est une amie qui l'a partagée avec moi, une amie très sage et très intelligente.

Tatie, merci. Merci pour ton soutien et pour ta compréhension.

Ari, j'imagine que les choses vont être encore un peu difficiles pendant quelque temps, mais ça va pas durer.

C'est une bonne idée, tatie.

Athéna, tu es prête ? Allons-y.

127

Hey there!
If you need help, or a friend needs help, tell someone. Find a trusted adult who can help, too. And, check out the resources below.
☮❤☺

Suicide and Crisis Lifeline
988 - via phone or text

The Crisis Text Line
Text TALK to 741741

The American Foundation for Suicide Prevention
https://afsp.org/get-help

Outside of the USA
Find a Helpline
https://findahelpline.com/i/iasp

127

GLOSSAIRE

A

à - to, at
abîme - abyss
aboyer - to bark
acheter - to buy
actuelle - current
admettre - to admit
adolescent.e -
    adolescent
adorable - adorable
adoré - adored
adulte(s) - adult(s)
agi - acted
ai - have
aide - helps
aident - help
aider - to help
aiderai - will help
aideront - will help
aidé - helped
aimais - liked
aime - like/s
aller - to go
allons - go
alors- so
ami/e - friend
améliorer - to
    improve
anxiété - anxiety
appartement -
    apartment
appelait - was calling
appeler - to call

appelles - call
après - after
argent - money
arrête - stop
arrêter - to stop
arrestation - arrest
arrivent - arrive
as - have
au - to/at the
aurais - would have
aurait - would have
aussi - also
automédication -
    self-medicate
autres - other
aux - to/at the
avaient - had
avais - had
avait - had
avant - before
avec - with
avenir - future

B

beaucoup - much, a
    lot
(avoir) besoin - to
    need
bien - well
bientôt - soon
blâme - blame
blâmer - to blame

blessure - injury
blesse - hurt
bloquer - to block
boîte - (small) box
boire - to drink
bonbons - candies
bonne - good
bourse - scholarship
bruit - noise
bu - drank
buvait - was drinking

C
c'/ça/ce - this
carton - (big) box
cause - cause
causé/e(s) - caused
cela - that
centre - center
certain - certain
cerveau - brain
ces - these
cet/tte - this
chambre - room
changer - to change
chaque - each
chemin - path
cher - expensive
chien - dog
chiot - puppy
chose(s) - thing(s)
claires - clear
client - client/
    customer
coût - cost

combien - how
    much/many
comme - like, as
commence - begin/s
commencé - began
comment - how
compliquées -
    complicated
compris - understood
comprehension -
    comprehension
compte - account
compétences - skills
compétition -
    competition
condo - condominium
confiance - trust
connaissais - knew
connaître - to know
conscients - aware
consument -
    consume
continuer - to
    continue
contrôle - control
contrôlent - control
corps - body
coupable - guilty
courage - courage
court - short
crime - crime
criminel - criminal

D
d'/de - of, from

dans - in
débarrasser - to get rid of
decisions - decisions
déesse - goddess
déjà - already
demande - ask/s
demandé - asked
depression - depression
déprime - depressed
dernière - last
des - of, from
destruction - destruction
détresse - distress
devoir - must
devrais - should
difficile(s) - difficult
difficultés - difficulties
dire - to say
directement - directly
dis - say
disparu - disappeared
dit - says
dois - must
dommage - shame
douloureux - painful
doute - doubt
du - of the
dur - hard
durer - to last

E

échapper - to escape
écoule - goes by
effondre - collapses
élaborons - elaborate
elle - she
elles - they
en - in, on
encore - again
enfant - child
enfin - finally
ensuite - next
entend - hears
entière - entire
entraîné - trained
entraîner - to train
entraînement(s) - training(s)
entre - between
entrouvre - opens
entrer - to enter
envoie - send
envoyé - sent
es - are
esprit - spirit
espérons - hopefully
essaie - try
est - is
et - and
étais - was
était - was
êtes - are
être - to be
étudié - studied

été - summer
évident - evident
exactement - exactly
examen - test
exemple - example

F

façon - way
faire - to do, make
fait - does, makes
fallait - had to
famille - family
fardeau - burden
fasses - do
faute - mistake
favoris - favorite
femelle - female
fin - end
final - final
financiers - financial
finit - ends
fois - time, instance
font - make, do
forces - strengths
formation - training
fort - strong
frère - brother
frais - fees
frappe - knocks

G

gagnais - won
gagner - to win
gentil - nice
gloire - glory

H

habitude - habit
heure - hour
heureuse - happy
hôpital - hospital

I

ici - here
idée(s) - idea(s)
il - he
ils - they
imagine - imagine/s
inférieur - inferior
inquiète - worried
intelligent - intelligent
internal - internal
inutile - useless
ira - will go

J

j'/je - I
jeune - young
jusqu' - until

L

l'/la/le - the
lâche - coward
laisse - leave/s
laisser - to leave
légèrement - slightly
leur(s) - their
lit - reads
lui - him
lumière - light

M

m'/me - me, to me
ma - my
mains - hands
maintenant - now
mais - but
maison - house
mal - badly
maman - mom
mauvaises - bad
maxime - saying
médicaments -
     medication
meilleur - better
mens - lie
mental - mental
mentir - to lie
mère - mother
merci - thank you
mes - my
met - put
mieux - better
mignonne - cute
mise - bet
moi - me
moins - less
moment - moment
mon - my
monde - world

N

n'/ne - not
ni - neither
nies - deny
niveau - level

nom - name
non - no

O

obligation -
     obligation
obscurité - darkness
obtenir - to get
on - we
ont - have
ou - or
oublier - to forget
oui - yes
ouvre - open/s
ouvrent - open
ouvrir - to open

P

papa - dad
par - by
parce que - because
parents - parents
parfaite - perfect
parlant - speaking
parle - speak/s
parler - speak
parlé - spoke
partagée - shared
participais -
     participated
participer - to
     participate
participé -
     participated
pas - not

passer - to pass
passé - passed
pauvre - poor
payer - to pay
(avoir de la) peine -
    to find it hard
pendant - during
penser - to think
penses - think
pensé/e(s) -
thought(s)
perfection -
    perfection
période - period
personne - person
perspective -
    perspective
petit - small
peu - little
peut - can
peuvent - can
peux - can
plan - plan
pleure - cries
pleurer - to cry
plus - more
police - police
porte - door
pose - puts
pour - for
pourquoi - why
pouvais - could
pouvait - could
pratiquer - to
    practice
pratiqué - practiced

préfère - prefer/s
préféré - preferred
prend - takes
prendre - to take
prends - take
présenté - presented
prête - ready
pris(es) - took
prison - prison
problème - problem
prochaine - next
programme -
    program
propre(s) - own
puis - then
puisse - may

Q
qu/que - that
quand - when
quartier -
    neighborhood
quelque - some
quelquefois -
    sometimes
qui - who
quoi - what

R
raison - reason
rappelle - remember
rationnellement -
    rationally
réel - real
réfléchir - to think

réfléchis - thinks
réfléchisses - reflect
regardait - was watching
regarde - watches
rentre - returns
réponse - answer
repose - rests
reproche - blame
responsable - responsible
reste - stay
retour - back
retourner - to return
réveille - wake/s up
rien - nothing
rongé - consumed

S

s'/se - to himself, herself
sage - wise
sagesse - wisdom
sais - know
sait - knows
sanglots - sobs
sans - without
saouler - to get drunk
saute - jump
savais - knew
savoir - to know
sciences - science
sens - sense
sentiments - feelings
sentir - to feel

sera - will be
serait - would be
seront - will be
ses - his, her
seul/e - alone
seulement - only
si - if
situation - situation
socialement - socially
sois - be
soit - either
soleil - sun
sombre - dark
son - his, her
sont - are
sorte - leave/s
sortir - to go out
soudain - suddenly
souffrir - to suffer
soutien - support
sport - sport
store - blinds
suis - am
suivant - following
supplie - beg
supplémentaire - supplementary/ additional
supporter - to bear
sur - on
surprise - surprise

T

t'/te - you, to/for you
ta - your
tais-toi - shut up
tait - silent
tante - aunt
tatie - auntie
tellement - such
temporaire - temporary
temps - time
(par) terre - on the floor
tes - your
texto - text
tiendront - will hold
tient - is holding
toi - you
ton - your
toujours - always
tous - all
tout/e(s) - all
très - very
tranquille - calm
travaillé - work
triste - sad
trouve - find/s
trouvée - found
tu - you

U

un/e - a, an
université - university

V

utile - useful

va - goes
vais - go
vas - go
venir - to come
verité - truth
verras - will see
vers - towards
veux - want
vie - life
visiter - to visit
vivre - to live
voir - to see
vois - see
volé - stolen
vont - go
voulais - wanted
voulait - wanted
vous - you (plural)
vrai - true
vraiment - truly

Y

y - there
yeux - eyes

146

ABOUT THE AUTHOR

Jennifer Degenhardt taught high school Spanish for over 20 years and now teaches at the college level. At the time she realized her own high school students, many of whom had learning challenges, acquired language best through stories, so she began to write ones that she thought would appeal to them. She has been writing ever since.

Other titles by Jen Degenhardt:

La chica nueva | *La Nouvelle Fille* | The New Girl | *Das Neue Mädchen* | *La nuova ragazza*
La chica nueva (the ancillary/workbook volume, Kindle book, audiobook)
Salida 8 | *Sortie no. 8*
Chuchotenango | *La terre des chiens errants* | *La vita dei cani*

139

Pesas / Poids et haltères /Weights and Dumbbells /Pesi

Luis, un soñador

El jersey / The Jersey / Le Maillot

La mochila /The Backpack / Le sac à dos

Moviendo montañas / Déplacer les montagnes /Moving Mountains / Spostando montagne

La vida es complicada / La vie est compliquée / Life is Complicated

La vida es complicada Practice & Questions (workbook)

El Mundial / La Coupe du Monde / The World Cup

Quince /Fifteen / Douze ans

Quince Practice & Questions (workbook)

El viaje difícil\ Un voyage difficile / A Difficult Journey

La niñera

¡¿Fútbol…americano?!\ Football…américain ?!

Era una chica nueva

Levantando pesas: un cuento en el pasado

Se movieron las montañas

Fue un viaje difícil

¿Qué pasó con el jersey?

Cuando se perdió la mochila

Con (un poco de) ayuda de mis amigos /With (a little) Help from My Friends / Un petit coup de main amical

Con (un po') d'aiuto dai miei amici

La última prueba / The Last Test

Los tres amigos / Three Friends / Drei Freunde / Les trois amis

140

La evolución musical
María María: un cuento de un huracán | María María: A
Story of a Storm | *Maria Maria: un histoire d'un orage*
Debido a la tormenta / Because of the Storm
La lucha de la vida / The Fight of His Life
Secretos / *Secrets*
Como vuela la pelota
Cambios / *Changements* / Changes
De la oscuridad a la luz
El pueblo | The Town

@JenniferDegenh

@jendegenhardt9

@PuentesLanguage &
World LanguageTeaching Stories (group)

Visit www.puenteslanguage.com to sign up to receive
information on new releases and other events.

Check out all titles as ebooks with audio on
www.digilangua.co.

ABOUT THE ILLUSTRATOR

Juliet Chattaway is a sixth-grade student at New Canaan Country School. She has loved art all her life and draws after school every day. In addition to drawing, Juliet spends her free time reading and writing short stories. One day, she hopes to publish her own Webtoon or book. Juliet lives in Darien, CT with her mother, father and younger brother, Nicholas.

ABOUT THE TRANSLATOR

Theresa Marrama has taught middle and high school French many years in upstate New York. A teacher certified in both French and Spanish, she teaches her classes using Comprehensible Input (CI). She is the author of several comprehensible novels in French, Spanish, German, Italian and English.

You can find all of her books on her website: www.compellinglanguagecorner.com and on the digital platform, www.digilangua.net.

ABOUT THE EDITORS

Françoise "Swaz" Piron was born and raised in Geneva, Switzerland, the daughter of a French mother and a Belgian father. She taught French (and German) at South Jefferson CSD for 35 years and retired in June 2021. She is a member of several world language teacher organizations, including ACTFL, NYSAFLT and AATF. She was a regular item writer and consultant at the NYS Education Department for the two French state exams for over 20 years. Swaz has presented numerous workshops at the local, state and national levels. She is the recipient of several NYSAFLT awards, was named "Chevalier dans L'Ordre des Palmes Académiques" by the French Ministry of Education and is the co-author of the book "*World Class, the Re-education of America*". When she is not proofreading or translating readers, she can be found doing outdoor activities, reading or working as a server in a local restaurant.

Nicole Piron is the translator's mother. She was born in Paris and spent her youth in the Bordeaux area. She has a degree in political science and English from la Sorbonne (Paris University) and was a translator for the United Nations in New York, where she worked for a few years. Nicole has always been active in her community, in local politics as a member of the "*conseil communal*" of the village of Coppet, Switzerland, as well as in the Catholic church of the town where she currently resides, Gland, Switzerland. When she is not helping her daughter proofread readers, she can be found reading, going to cultural events and visiting with her network of friends.

www.ingramcontent.com/pod-product-compliance
Lightning Source LLC
Chambersburg PA
CBHW071222090426
42736CB00014B/2938